DIAB...
Main Dishes

beef
& pork

Tex-Mex Flank Steak Salad

½ beef flank steak (about 6 ounces)
½ teaspoon Mexican seasoning or chili powder
⅛ teaspoon salt
   Olive oil cooking spray
4 cups packaged mixed salad greens
1 can (11 ounces) mandarin orange segments, drained
2 tablespoons green taco sauce

1. Cut flank steak lengthwise in half, then crosswise into thin strips. Combine steak, seasoning and salt in medium bowl; toss to coat.

2. Lightly spray large skillet with cooking spray; heat over medium-high heat. Add steak; cook and stir 1 to 2 minutes or until desired doneness.

3. Toss together greens and orange segments. Arrange on serving plates. Top with warm steak; drizzle with taco sauce.

Makes 2 servings

Nutrients per Serving (½ of total recipe):
Calories: 240, **Calories from Fat:** 25%, **Total Fat:** 7g,
Saturated Fat: 3g, **Cholesterol:** 37mg, **Sodium:** 388mg,
Carbohydrate: 21g, **Dietary Fiber:** 2g, **Protein:** 25g

Dietary Exchanges: ½ Fruit, 2½ Vegetable, 2½ Lean Meat

Pork and Plum Kabobs

¾ pound boneless pork loin chops (1 inch thick),
  trimmed of fat and cut into 1-inch pieces
1½ teaspoons ground cumin
½ teaspoon ground cinnamon
¼ teaspoon salt
¼ teaspoon garlic powder
¼ teaspoon ground red pepper
¼ cup sliced green onions
¼ cup red raspberry fruit spread
1 tablespoon orange juice
3 plums, pitted and cut into wedges

1. Place pork in large resealable food storage bag. Combine cumin, cinnamon, salt, garlic powder and red pepper in small bowl; sprinkle over meat in bag. Shake to coat meat with spices.

2. Prepare grill for direct cooking. Combine green onions, raspberry fruit spread and orange juice in small bowl; set aside.

3. Alternately thread pork and plum wedges onto 8 skewers.* Grill kabobs over medium heat 12 to 14 minutes or until pork is barely pink in center, turning once. Brush frequently with raspberry mixture during last 5 minutes of grilling.   *Makes 4 servings*

If using wooden skewers, soak in water 20 minutes before using to prevent burning.

Prep Time: 10 minutes
Grill Time: 12 to 14 minutes

Nutrients per Serving (2 kabobs):
Calories: 191, **Calories from Fat:** 23%, **Total Fat:** 5g,
Saturated Fat: 2g, **Cholesterol:** 53mg, **Sodium:** 183mg,
Carbohydrate: 17g, **Dietary Fiber:** 1g, **Protein:** 19g

Dietary Exchanges: 1 Fruit, 2½ Lean Meat

Favorite Beef Stew

3 medium carrots, cut lengthwise in half, then cut into 1-inch pieces
3 stalks celery, cut into 1-inch pieces
2 large potatoes, peeled and cut into ½-inch pieces
1½ cups chopped onions
3 cloves garlic, chopped
4½ teaspoons Worcestershire sauce
¾ teaspoon *each* dried thyme and dried basil
½ teaspoon black pepper
1 bay leaf
2 pounds beef stew meat (1-inch pieces)
1 can (about 14 ounces) diced tomatoes
1 can (about 14 ounces) fat-free reduced-sodium beef broth
½ cup cold water
¼ cup all-purpose flour

SLOW COOKER DIRECTIONS

1. Layer ingredients in slow cooker in the following order: carrots, celery, potatoes, onions, garlic, Worcestershire sauce, thyme, basil, pepper, bay leaf, beef, tomatoes and broth. Cover and cook on LOW 8 to 9 hours.

2. Remove beef and vegetables to large serving bowl; cover and keep warm. Remove and discard bay leaf.

3. Increase heat to HIGH. Blend water and flour in small bowl until smooth. Add ½ cup cooking liquid; mix well. Stir flour mixture into slow cooker. Cover and cook 15 minutes or until thickened. Pour sauce over meat and vegetables. Serve immediately.

Makes 8 servings

Nutrients per Serving (⅛ of total recipe):
Calories: 276, **Calories from Fat:** 20%, **Total Fat:** 8g,
Saturated Fat: 3g, **Cholesterol:** 70mg, **Sodium:** 266mg,
Carbohydrate: 25g, **Dietary Fiber:** 3g, **Protein:** 25g

Dietary Exchanges: 1 Starch, 1½ Vegetable, 3 Lean Meat

Butternut Gratin

1 butternut squash
6 ounces lean boneless pork chops, trimmed of fat,
   cooked and cut into bite-size pieces
½ cup chopped celery
½ cup vegetable broth
⅓ cup whole grain dry bread crumbs
¼ cup sliced green onions
2 tablespoons shredded reduced-fat Cheddar cheese
¼ teaspoon black pepper (optional)

MICROWAVE DIRECTIONS

1. Pierce squash with knife tip in several places. Microwave on HIGH 15 to 20 minutes or until squash is barely tender.

2. Remove squash from microwave and let stand about 5 minutes or until cool enough to handle. Cut off top and discard. Slice squash in half lengthwise and scoop out seeds. Use knife to score each half into a grid of 1-inch cubes, leaving skin intact; cut cubes from skin.

3. Lightly coat medium microwavable dish with nonstick cooking spray. Combine squash, pork, celery, broth, bread crumbs and green onions in prepared dish. Top with cheese. Microwave on HIGH 2 to 2½ minutes or until squash is tender and heated through. Season with pepper, if desired.

Makes 2 servings

Nutrients per Serving (1¾ cups Butternut Gratin):
Calories: 285, **Calories from Fat:** 25%, **Total Fat:** 8g,
Saturated Fat: 3g, **Cholesterol:** 83mg, **Sodium:** 452mg,
Carbohydrate: 23g, **Dietary Fiber:** 5g, **Protein:** 31g

Dietary Exchanges: 1½ Starch, ½ Vegetable, 3½ Lean Meat

Stuffed Eggplant

Nonstick cooking spray
2 eggplants (about 8 ounces each), halved lengthwise
½ teaspoon salt
1½ teaspoons chopped garlic
1 teaspoon black pepper
1 pound boneless beef sirloin steak, trimmed of
   visible fat and cut into ¼-inch strips
2 cups sliced red and/or green bell peppers
2 cups sliced mushrooms
¼ cup water
Pinch paprika and chopped fresh parsley (optional)

1. Preheat oven to 450°F. Spray large baking dish with cooking spray.

2. Place eggplant halves, cut sides up, in prepared baking dish; pierce with fork in approximately 8 places. Sprinkle each eggplant half with ⅛ teaspoon salt. Cover with foil; bake 45 minutes.

3. Meanwhile, spray large nonstick skillet with cooking spray; heat over medium heat. Add garlic and black pepper; cook and stir 2 minutes. Add steak; cook and stir 5 minutes.

4. Add bell peppers; cook 5 minutes. Add mushrooms; cook 5 minutes. Stir in water; cover. Remove skillet from heat.

5. Remove eggplant from oven; let cool 5 minutes. Mash cooked eggplant centers with fork without breaking shells. Top each half with steak mixture; combine with mashed eggplant. Cover with foil; bake 15 minutes. Garnish with paprika and parsley. *Makes 4 servings*

Nutrients per Serving (1 stuffed eggplant half):
Calories: 195, **Calories from Fat:** 23%, **Total Fat:** 5g,
Saturated Fat: 2g, **Sodium:** 348mg, **Carbohydrate:** 12g,
Dietary Fiber: 4g, **Protein:** 25g

Dietary Exchanges: 2½ Vegetable, 2½ Lean Meat

Browned Pork Chops with Gravy

½ teaspoon *each* dried sage and dried marjoram
¼ teaspoon black pepper
⅛ teaspoon salt
4 boneless pork loin chops (about ¼ pound each),
   trimmed of fat
   Olive oil cooking spray
¼ cup chopped onion
1 clove garlic, minced
1 cup sliced mushrooms
¾ cup beef broth
⅓ cup fat-free sour cream
1 tablespoon all-purpose flour
1 teaspoon Dijon mustard
2 cups hot cooked yolk-free wide egg noodles
   Chopped fresh parsley (optional)

1. Combine sage, marjoram, pepper and salt in small bowl. Rub onto both sides of pork chops. Spray large nonstick skillet with cooking spray; heat over medium heat. Add pork; cook 5 minutes or until just barely pink in center, turning once. Remove from skillet; keep warm.

2. Add onion and garlic to skillet; cook and stir 2 minutes. Add mushrooms and broth. Bring to a boil over high heat. Reduce heat; simmer, covered, 3 to 4 minutes or until mushrooms are tender.

3. Whisk together sour cream, flour and mustard in small bowl. Whisk in about 3 tablespoons broth mixture from skillet. Stir sour cream mixture into skillet. Cook, stirring constantly, until mixture comes to a boil. Serve gravy over pork chops and noodles. Garnish with parsley.   *Makes 4 servings*

Nutrients per Serving (1 pork chop with ½ cup noodles and ¼ cup gravy):
Calories: 315, **Calories from Fat:** 29%, **Total Fat:** 10g, **Saturated Fat:** 3g, **Cholesterol:** 67mg, **Sodium:** 296mg, **Carbohydrate:** 30g, **Dietary Fiber:** 2g, **Protein:** 25g

Dietary Exchanges: 1½ Starch, 1 Vegetable, 2½ Lean Meat

Browned Pork Chop with Gravy

Grilled Flank Steak with Horseradish Sauce

- 1 beef flank steak (about 1 pound)
- 2 tablespoons reduced-sodium soy sauce
- 1 tablespoon red wine vinegar
- 2 cloves garlic, minced
- ½ teaspoon black pepper
- 1 cup fat-free sour cream
- ¼ cup finely chopped fresh parsley
- 1 tablespoon prepared horseradish
- 1 tablespoon Dijon mustard
- ½ teaspoon salt
- 6 sourdough rolls (2 ounces each), split
  Romaine lettuce

1. Place flank steak in large resealable food storage bag. Add soy sauce, vinegar, garlic and pepper. Close bag securely; turn to coat. Marinate in refrigerator at least 1 hour.

2. Prepare grill for direct cooking. Drain steak; discard marinade. Grill steak over medium heat, uncovered, 17 to 21 minutes for medium-rare to medium or until desired doneness, turning once. Remove from grill. Cover steak with foil; let stand 15 minutes. Thinly slice steak across the grain.

3. Combine sour cream, parsley, horseradish, mustard and salt in small bowl until well blended. Spread rolls with horseradish sauce; layer with sliced steak and lettuce.

Makes 6 servings

Nutrients per Serving (1 sandwich [1 roll with 2 ounces cooked beef, 3 tablespoons plus 1 teaspoon horseradish sauce and lettuce]):
Calories: 307, **Calories from Fat:** 27%, **Total Fat:** 9g,
Saturated Fat: 3g, **Cholesterol:** 32mg, **Sodium:** 600mg,
Carbohydrate: 29g, **Dietary Fiber:** 1g, **Protein:** 24g

Dietary Exchanges: 2 Starch, 3 Lean Meat

Szechwan Pork Stir-Fry over Spinach

2 teaspoons sesame oil, divided
¾ cup matchstick-size carrot strips
½ pound pork tenderloin, halved and thinly sliced
3 cloves garlic, minced
2 teaspoons minced bottled or fresh ginger
¼ to ½ teaspoon red pepper flakes
1 tablespoon mirin* or dry sherry
1 tablespoon reduced-sodium soy sauce
2 teaspoons cornstarch
8 ounces baby spinach
2 teaspoons toasted sesame seeds

*Mirin, a sweet wine made from rice, is an essential flavoring in Japanese cuisine. It is available in Asian markets and the Asian or gourmet section of some supermarkets.

1. Heat 1 teaspoon oil in large nonstick skillet over medium-high heat. Add carrot strips; cook 3 minutes, stirring occasionally. Add pork, garlic, ginger and red pepper flakes. Stir-fry 3 minutes or until pork is no longer pink. Stir mirin and soy sauce into cornstarch in small bowl until smooth; add to skillet. Cook and stir 1 minute or until sauce thickens.

2. Heat remaining 1 teaspoon oil in medium saucepan over medium-high heat. Add spinach. Cover and cook 1 minute. Uncover and turn spinach with tongs. Cover and cook 1 minute or until spinach is barely wilted. Transfer spinach to serving plates. Spoon pork mixture over spinach. Sprinkle with sesame seeds. *Makes 2 servings*

Nutrients per Serving (½ of total recipe):
Calories: 256, **Calories from Fat:** 35%, **Total Fat:** 10g, **Saturated Fat:** 2g, **Cholesterol:** 73mg, **Sodium:** 466mg, **Carbohydrate:** 11g, **Dietary Fiber:** 3g, **Protein:** 29g

Dietary Exchanges: 2 Vegetable, 3½ Lean Meat

O K

Yankee Pot Roast and Vegetables

1 beef chuck pot roast (2½ pounds), trimmed of
   visible fat and cut into 2-inch pieces
   Salt and black pepper (optional)
3 ~~unpeeled~~ medium baking potatoes (about 1 pound),
   cut into quarters
2 large carrots, cut into ¾-inch slices
2 stalks celery, cut into 1-inch slices
¼ ~~1~~ medium onion, sliced
1 large parsnip, cut into ¾-inch slices (optional)
2 bay leaves
1 teaspoon dried rosemary   more spice
½ teaspoon dried thyme   (vary)
½ cup reduced-sodium beef broth
   (use (artenkind))

SLOW COOKER DIRECTIONS use all

1. Season beef with salt and pepper, if desired.

2. Combine vegetables, bay leaves, rosemary and thyme
in slow cooker. Place beef on top of vegetables. Pour broth
over beef. Cover; cook on LOW 8½ to 9 hours or until beef is
fork-tender.

3. Transfer beef to serving platter. Arrange vegetables
around beef. Remove and discard bay leaves.

Makes 10 servings

Note: To make gravy, ladle the juices into a 2-cup measure;
let stand 5 minutes. Skim off and discard fat. Measure
remaining juices and heat to a boil in small saucepan. For
each cup of juice, mix 2 tablespoons of flour with ¼ cup of
cold water until smooth. Stir flour mixture into boiling juices,
stirring constantly, 1 minute or until thickened.

Nutrients per Serving (¹⁄₁₀ of total recipe [without salt and
pepper seasoning]):
Calories: 270, **Calories from Fat:** 33%, **Total Fat:** 10g,
Saturated Fat: 4g, **Cholesterol:** 75mg, **Sodium:** 99mg,
Carbohydrate: 15g, **Dietary Fiber:** 3g, **Protein:** 28g

Dietary Exchanges: 1 Starch, 3½ Lean Meat

Potato and Pork Frittata

12 ounces (about 3 cups) frozen hash brown potatoes
 1 teaspoon Cajun seasoning
 4 egg whites
 2 eggs
 ¼ cup low-fat (1%) milk
 1 teaspoon dry mustard
 ¼ teaspoon black pepper
10 ounces (about 3 cups) frozen stir-fry vegetable blend
 ⅓ cup water
 ¾ cup chopped cooked lean pork
 ½ cup (2 ounces) shredded reduced-fat Cheddar cheese

1. Preheat oven to 400°F. Spray baking sheet with nonstick cooking spray. Spread potatoes on baking sheet; sprinkle with seasoning. Bake 15 minutes or until heated through. Remove from oven. *Reduce oven temperature to 350°F.*

2. Beat egg whites, eggs, milk, mustard and pepper in small bowl. Place vegetables and water in medium ovenproof nonstick skillet. Cook over medium heat 5 minutes or until vegetables are crisp-tender; drain.

3. Add pork and potatoes to vegetables in skillet; stir to blend. Add egg mixture. Sprinkle with cheese. Cook over medium-low heat 5 minutes. Place skillet in 350°F oven and bake 5 minutes or until egg mixture is set and cheese is melted. Cut into 4 wedges. *Makes 4 servings*

Nutrients per Serving (1 frittata wedge [¼ of total recipe]):
Calories: 268, **Calories from Fat:** 37%, **Total Fat:** 11g, **Saturated Fat:** 5g, **Cholesterol:** 145mg, **Sodium:** 258mg, **Carbohydrate:** 20g, **Dietary Fiber:** 2g, **Protein:** 22g

Dietary Exchanges: 1½ Starch, 2 Lean Meat, 1 Fat

chicken

Autumn Pasta

1 boneless skinless chicken breast (about ¼ pound),
  cut into ½-inch cubes
1 large fennel bulb, trimmed, quartered and sliced
  (1½ to 2 cups)
8 brussels sprouts, trimmed and halved
2 medium tomatoes, chopped
¼ cup lemon juice
1 tablespoon olive oil
1 teaspoon bottled minced garlic
  Nonstick cooking spray
1 cup cooked whole grain rotini pasta
2 tablespoons shredded Parmesan cheese

1. Combine chicken, fennel, brussels sprouts, tomatoes, lemon juice, olive oil and garlic in large bowl.

2. Lightly coat large skillet with cooking spray; heat over medium heat. Add chicken mixture; cook, covered, 15 minutes or until chicken is cooked through and vegetables are tender.

3. Add pasta to skillet; cook and stir until heated through. Sprinkle with cheese before serving.   *Makes 2 servings*

Nutrients per Serving (½ of total recipe):
Calories: 315, **Calories from Fat:** 26%, **Total Fat:** 10g,
Saturated Fat: 2g, **Cholesterol:** 37mg, **Sodium:** 168mg,
Carbohydrate: 38g, **Dietary Fiber:** 9g, **Protein:** 23g

Dietary Exchanges: 1½ Starch, 3 Vegetable, 2 Lean Meat, ½ Fat

Double-Quick Mozzarella Chicken

4 boneless skinless chicken breasts (about ¼ pound each)
½ medium lemon or lime
1 teaspoon ground cumin
¼ teaspoon salt
¾ cup (3 ounces) shredded reduced-fat mozzarella cheese
½ (10-ounce) can Mexican-style diced tomatoes with green chiles,* drained
2 tablespoons chopped fresh cilantro (optional)

Reserve remaining tomatoes for another use.

1. Preheat oven to 400°F. Coat baking sheet with nonstick cooking spray. Arrange chicken on baking sheet about 2 inches apart. Squeeze lemon over chicken; sprinkle with cumin and salt. Bake 20 minutes.

2. Sprinkle cheese evenly over chicken; bake 5 minutes or until chicken is no longer pink in center. Transfer chicken to serving platter. Spoon about 3 tablespoons tomatoes over each chicken breast. Garnish with cilantro.

Makes 4 servings

Nutrients per Serving (1 breast topped with cheese and tomatoes):
Calories: 197, **Calories from Fat:** 27%, **Total Fat:** 6g,
Saturated Fat: 2g, **Cholesterol:** 70mg, **Sodium:** 490mg,
Carbohydrate: 4g, **Dietary Fiber:** 1g, **Protein:** 29g.

Dietary Exchanges: ½ Vegetable, 3½ Lean Meat

Chicken Chow Mein

1 pound boneless skinless chicken breasts, cut into thin strips
2 cloves garlic, minced
1 teaspoon vegetable oil, divided
2 tablespoons dry sherry
2 tablespoons reduced-sodium soy sauce
6 ounces (about 2 cups) fresh snow peas, cut in half crosswise *or* 1 package (6 ounces) frozen snow peas, thawed
3 green onions, cut diagonally into 1-inch pieces
4 ounces uncooked Chinese egg noodles or vermicelli, cooked and drained
1 teaspoon dark sesame oil (optional)
Chopped seeded tomato (optional)

1. Toss chicken and garlic in medium bowl.

2. Heat ½ teaspoon vegetable oil in wok or large skillet over medium-high heat. Add chicken mixture; stir-fry 3 minutes or until chicken is no longer pink. Transfer to medium bowl; toss with sherry and soy sauce.

3. Heat remaining ½ teaspoon vegetable oil in wok. Add snow peas; stir-fry 2 minutes (1 minute if using frozen). Add green onions; stir-fry 30 seconds. Add chicken mixture; stir-fry 1 minute or until chicken is cooked through.

4. Add noodles to wok; stir-fry 2 minutes or until heated through. Stir in sesame oil, if desired. Garnish with tomato.

Makes 4 servings

Nutrients per Serving (1 cup chow mein):
Calories: 252, **Calories from Fat:** 10%, **Total Fat:** 3g,
Saturated Fat: 1g, **Cholesterol:** 66mg, **Sodium:** 461mg,
Carbohydrate: 22g, **Dietary Fiber:** 2g, **Protein:** 31g

Dietary Exchanges: 1 Starch, 1 Vegetable, 3 Lean Meat

Family-Style Creamy Chicken and Noodles

    8 ounces uncooked yolk-free wide egg noodles
    4 cups water
    1 pound boneless skinless chicken breasts
 1½ cups chopped onions
    ¾ cup chopped celery
    ½ teaspoon salt
    ½ teaspoon dried thyme
    1 bay leaf
    ⅛ teaspoon white pepper
    1 can (10¾ ounces) condensed cream of chicken
       soup, undiluted
    ½ cup buttermilk
       Chopped fresh parsley (optional)

1. Cook pasta according to package directions, omitting salt. Drain; set aside.

2. Meanwhile, bring water to a boil in large saucepan over high heat. Add chicken, onions, celery, salt, thyme, bay leaf and white pepper. Return to a boil. Reduce heat to low; simmer, uncovered, 35 minutes. Remove chicken; cut into ½-inch pieces. Set aside.

3. Increase heat to high. Return liquid in saucepan to a boil. Continue cooking until liquid and vegetables have reduced to 1 cup. Remove from heat; discard bay leaf. Whisk in soup and buttermilk until well blended. Add chicken pieces and pasta; toss to blend. Garnish with parsley.

Makes 6 servings

Nutrients per Serving (⅙ of total recipe):
Calories: 289, **Calories from Fat:** 22%, **Total Fat:** 7g,
Saturated Fat: 2g, **Cholesterol:** 74mg, **Sodium:** 669mg,
Carbohydrate: 33g, **Dietary Fiber:** 2g, **Protein:** 22g

Dietary Exchanges: 2 Starch, ½ Vegetable, 2 Lean Meat

Creole Vegetables and Chicken

Nonstick cooking spray
1 can (about 14 ounces) no-salt-added diced tomatoes
8 ounces frozen cut okra
2 cups chopped green bell peppers
1 cup chopped yellow onions
1 cup fat-free reduced-sodium chicken broth
¾ cup sliced celery
2 teaspoons Worcestershire sauce
1 teaspoon dried thyme
1 bay leaf
1 pound chicken tenders, cut into bite-size pieces
1 tablespoon olive oil
1½ teaspoons sugar substitute
¾ teaspoon Cajun seasoning
Hot pepper sauce (optional)
¼ cup chopped fresh parsley

SLOW COOKER DIRECTIONS

1. Coat 3½- to 4-quart slow cooker with cooking spray. Add tomatoes, okra, bell peppers, onions, broth, celery, Worcestershire sauce, thyme and bay leaf. Cover; cook on LOW 9 hours or on HIGH 4½ hours.

2. Coat large nonstick skillet with cooking spray. Add chicken; cook, stirring frequently, over medium-high heat 6 minutes or until lightly browned. Add to slow cooker with oil, sugar substitute, seasoning and hot pepper sauce, if desired. Increase slow cooker temperature to HIGH. Cook on HIGH 15 minutes; add parsley. *Makes 4 servings*

Nutrients per Serving (1½ cups):
Calories: 190, **Calories from Fat:** 23%, **Total Fat:** 6g,
Saturated Fat: 1g, **Cholesterol:** 42mg, **Sodium:** 174mg,
Carbohydrate: 18g, **Dietary Fiber:** 6g, **Protein:** 20g

Dietary Exchanges: 3½ Vegetable, 2½ Lean Meat

Creole Vegetables and Chicken

Sassy Chicken & Peppers

- 2 teaspoons Mexican seasoning*
- 2 boneless skinless chicken breasts (about ¼ pound each)
- 2 teaspoons vegetable oil
- 1 small red onion, sliced
- ½ medium red bell pepper, cut into thin strips
- ½ medium yellow or green bell pepper, cut into thin strips
- ¼ cup chunky salsa or chipotle salsa
- 1 tablespoon lime juice
  Lime wedges (optional)

If Mexican seasoning is not available, substitute with a blend of 1 teaspoon chili powder, ½ teaspoon ground cumin, ½ teaspoon salt and ⅛ teaspoon ground red pepper.

1. Sprinkle seasoning over both sides of chicken; set aside.

2. Heat oil in large nonstick skillet over medium heat. Add onion; cook 3 minutes, stirring occasionally.

3. Add bell peppers; cook 3 minutes, stirring occasionally. Stir salsa and lime juice into vegetables.

4. Push vegetables to edge of skillet. Add chicken to skillet. Cook 5 minutes; turn. Cook 4 minutes or until chicken is no longer pink in center and vegetables are tender.

5. Transfer chicken to serving plates; top with vegetable mixture. Garnish with lime wedges. *Makes 2 servings*

Nutrients per Serving (½ of total recipe):
Calories: 224, **Calories from Fat:** 31%, **Total Fat:** 8g,
Saturated Fat: 1g, **Cholesterol:** 69mg, **Sodium:** 813mg,
Carbohydrate: 11g, **Dietary Fiber:** 3g, **Protein:** 27g

Dietary Exchanges: 2 Vegetable, 3 Lean Meat

Chicken & Spinach Quesadillas with Pico de Gallo

- 2 cups chopped seeded tomatoes, divided
- 1 cup chopped green onions, divided
- ½ cup chopped fresh cilantro
- 1 tablespoon minced jalapeño pepper*
- 1 tablespoon lime juice
  Nonstick cooking spray
- 10 (8-inch) fat-free flour tortillas
- 1 cup packed chopped stemmed spinach
- 1 cup shredded cooked boneless skinless chicken breast
- ¾ cup shredded reduced-fat Cheddar cheese

*Jalapeño peppers can sting and irritate the skin, so wear rubber gloves when handling peppers and do not touch your eyes.

1. For Pico de Gallo, mix 1½ cups tomatoes, ¾ cup green onions, cilantro, jalapeño pepper and lime juice in medium bowl.

2. Spray large nonstick skillet with cooking spray; heat over medium heat. Sprinkle tortilla with water; place in skillet. Cook 20 to 30 seconds or until hot, turning once. Repeat with remaining tortillas.

3. Divide remaining ½ cup tomatoes, ¼ cup green onions, spinach and chicken among 5 tortillas; sprinkle with cheese. Top with remaining 5 tortillas.

4. Cook quesadillas in same skillet, 1 at a time, over medium heat 2 minutes per side or until cheese is melted. Cut quesadillas into wedges; serve with Pico de Gallo.

Makes 5 servings

Nutrients per Serving (1 quesadilla with ½ cup plus 1½ teaspoons Pico de Gallo):
Calories: 240, **Calories from Fat:** 18%, **Total Fat:** 5g, **Saturated Fat:** 5g, **Cholesterol:** 34mg, **Sodium:** 540mg, **Carbohydrate:** 32g, **Dietary Fiber:** 14g, **Protein:** 18g

Dietary Exchanges: 2 Starch, 1½ Lean Meat

Grilled Chicken Adobo

½ cup chopped onion
⅓ cup lime juice
6 cloves garlic, coarsely chopped
1 teaspoon ground cumin
1 teaspoon dried oregano
½ teaspoon dried thyme
¼ teaspoon ground red pepper
6 boneless skinless chicken breasts (about ¼ pound each)
3 tablespoons chopped fresh cilantro (optional)

1. Combine onion, lime juice and garlic in food processor. Process until onion is finely minced. Transfer to resealable food storage bag. Add cumin, oregano, thyme and red pepper; knead bag until blended. Place chicken in bag; press out air and seal. Turn to coat chicken with marinade. Refrigerate 30 minutes or up to 4 hours.

2. Spray grid with nonstick cooking spray. Prepare grill for direct cooking. Remove chicken from marinade; discard marinade. Place chicken on prepared grid 3 to 4 inches from medium-hot coals. Grill 5 to 7 minutes per side or until chicken is no longer pink in center. Garnish with cilantro.

Makes 6 servings

Nutrients per Serving (1 grilled chicken breast):
Calories: 139, **Calories from Fat:** 19%, **Total Fat:** 3g,
Saturated Fat: <1g, **Cholesterol:** 69mg, **Sodium:** 61mg,
Carbohydrate: 1g, **Dietary Fiber:** <1g, **Protein:** 25g

Dietary Exchanges: 3 Lean Meat

fish
& shellfish

Beijing Fillet of Sole

2 tablespoons reduced-sodium soy sauce
2 teaspoons dark sesame oil
4 sole fillets (about 6 ounces each)
1¼ cups shredded cabbage or coleslaw mix
½ cup crushed chow mein noodles
1 egg white, lightly beaten
2 teaspoons sesame seeds

1. Preheat oven to 350°F. Combine soy sauce and oil in small bowl. Place sole in shallow dish. Lightly brush both sides of sole with soy sauce mixture.

2. Combine cabbage, noodles, egg white and remaining soy sauce mixture in medium bowl. Spoon evenly down center of each fillet. Roll up fillets. Place seam side down in shallow foil-lined baking pan.

3. Sprinkle rolls with sesame seeds. Bake 25 to 30 minutes or until fish begins to flake when tested with fork.

Makes 4 servings

Nutrients per Serving (1 roll):
Calories: 252, **Calories from Fat:** 29%, **Total Fat:** 8g,
Saturated Fat: 1g, **Cholesterol:** 80mg, **Sodium:** 435mg,
Carbohydrate: 6g, **Dietary Fiber:** <1g, **Protein:** 34g

Dietary Exchanges: 1½ Vegetable, 4 Lean Meat

Savoy Shrimp

1 pound large raw shrimp, peeled and deveined
  (with tails on)
½ teaspoon Chinese 5-spice powder*
2 tablespoons dark sesame oil
4 cups sliced savoy or napa cabbage
1 cup snow peas, trimmed
1 tablespoon diced candied ginger (optional)
1 tablespoon reduced-sodium soy sauce
1 teaspoon red pepper flakes
½ teaspoon ground ginger
  Juice of 1 lime
¼ cup chopped fresh cilantro (optional)

Chinese 5-spice powder is a blend of cinnamon, cloves, fennel seed, anise and Szechwan peppercorns. It is available in most supermarkets and at Asian grocery stores.

1. Place shrimp in colander and rinse well; drain. Toss with Chinese 5-spice powder in medium bowl. Set aside.

2. Heat oil in 12-inch nonstick skillet over medium heat. Add cabbage, snow peas, candied ginger, if desired, soy sauce, red pepper flakes and ground ginger. Cook, stirring often, until cabbage is tender.

3. Add shrimp and lime juice; stir to blend. Cover skillet and reduce heat to low. Cook 3 minutes or until shrimp are pink and opaque. Garnish with cilantro.   *Makes 4 servings*

Nutrients per Serving (5 shrimp with 1 cup vegetables):
Calories: 234, **Calories from Fat:** 37%, **Total Fat:** 9g,
Saturated Fat: 1g, **Cholesterol:** 172mg, **Sodium:** 318mg,
Carbohydrate: 12g, **Dietary Fiber:** 3g, **Protein:** 25g

Dietary Exchanges: 2 Vegetable, 3 Lean Meat

Salmon-Potato Cakes with Mustard Tartar Sauce

3 unpeeled small red potatoes (about 8 ounces)
1 cup cooked flaked salmon
1 egg white
2 green onions, chopped
1 tablespoon chopped fresh parsley
½ teaspoon Cajun or Creole seasoning
1 teaspoon olive or canola oil

MUSTARD TARTAR SAUCE
1 tablespoon reduced-fat mayonnaise
1 tablespoon plain fat-free yogurt or fat-free sour cream
2 teaspoons coarse grain mustard
1 tablespoon chopped fresh parsley
1 tablespoon chopped dill pickle
1 teaspoon lemon juice

1. Halve potatoes; place in small saucepan with ½ cup water. Bring to a boil over high heat. Reduce heat; simmer 15 minutes or until potatoes are tender. Drain; mash potatoes with fork.

2. Combine mashed potatoes, salmon, egg white, green onions, parsley and seasoning in medium bowl.

3. Heat oil in large nonstick skillet over medium heat. Turn ½ cup salmon mixture out into skillet; flatten slightly. Repeat for second cake. Cook 7 minutes or until browned, turning once. Meanwhile, combine all sauce ingredients in small bowl. Serve cakes with sauce. *Makes 2 servings*

Nutrients per Serving (1 cake with 2 tablespoons sauce):
Calories: 276, **Calories from Fat:** 37%, **Total Fat:** 11g,
Saturated Fat: 2g, **Cholesterol:** 52mg, **Sodium:** 300mg,
Carbohydrate: 24g, **Dietary Fiber:** 2g, **Protein:** 19g

Dietary Exchanges: 1½ Starch, 2 Lean Meat, 1 Fat

Southwest Roasted Salmon & Corn

2 medium ears fresh corn, unhusked
1 salmon fillet (about 6 ounces), cut in half
1 tablespoon plus 1 teaspoon lime juice, divided
1 clove garlic, minced
½ teaspoon chili powder
¼ teaspoon *each* ground cumin and dried oregano
⅛ teaspoon salt, divided
⅛ teaspoon black pepper
2 teaspoons margarine, melted
2 teaspoons minced fresh cilantro

1. Preheat oven to 400°F. Spray shallow 1-quart baking dish with nonstick cooking spray.

2. Pull back corn husks, leaving attached. Discard silk. Bring husks back up over each ear. Soak corn in cold water 20 minutes.

3. Place salmon, skin side down, in prepared dish; drizzle with 1 tablespoon lime juice. Marinate at room temperature 15 minutes.

4. Combine garlic, chili powder, cumin, oregano, half of salt and pepper in small bowl. Pat salmon lightly with paper towel. Rub garlic mixture on salmon.

5. Place corn on one side of oven rack. Roast 10 minutes; turn.

6. Place salmon in baking dish on other side of oven rack. Roast 15 minutes or until salmon begins to flake when tested with fork and corn is tender.

7. Combine margarine, cilantro, remaining 1 teaspoon lime juice and remaining salt in small bowl. Remove husks from corn. Brush lime mixture over corn. Serve corn with salmon.

Makes 2 servings

Note: Corn can also be cooked in boiling water. Omit steps 2 and 5. Husk the corn and place in a large pot of boiling water. Cover; remove from heat and let stand for 10 minutes. Drain and brush with lime mixture. Serve corn with salmon.

Nutrients per Serving (1 salmon fillet half with 1 ear of corn):
Calories: 186, **Calories from Fat:** 29%, **Total Fat:** 6g,
Saturated Fat: 1g, **Cholesterol:** 43mg, **Sodium:** 243mg,
Carbohydrate: 16g, **Dietary Fiber:** 2g, **Protein:** 19g

Dietary Exchanges: 1 Starch, 2 Lean Meat

Broiled Scallops with Honey-Lime Marinade

- **2 tablespoons honey**
- **4 teaspoons lime juice**
- **1 tablespoon vegetable oil**
- **¼ teaspoon grated lime peel**
- **¼ teaspoon salt**
- **1 dash hot pepper sauce**
- **½ pound bay, calico or sea scallops**
- **1 lime, cut into wedges**

Combine honey, lime juice, oil, lime peel, salt and hot pepper sauce in large bowl. Rinse scallops and pat dry with paper towel; add to marinade. Marinate scallops in refrigerator, stirring occasionally, 1 hour or overnight. Preheat broiler. Arrange scallops and marinade in single layer on 2 broiler-proof pans. Broil 4 inches from heat source 4 to 7 minutes or until opaque and lightly browned. Serve with lime wedges. *Makes 2 servings*

Favorite recipe from **National Honey Board**

Nutrients per Serving (½ of total recipe):
Calories: 239, **Calories from Fat:** 30%, **Total Fat:** 8g,
Saturated Fat: 1g, **Cholesterol:** 48mg, **Sodium:** 533mg,
Carbohydrate: 23g, **Dietary Fiber:** 1g, **Protein:** 21g

Dietary Exchanges: 1½ Fruit, 3 Lean Meat

Skillet Fish with Lemon Tarragon "Butter"

4 teaspoons lemon juice, divided
2 teaspoons reduced-fat margarine
½ teaspoon grated lemon peel
¼ teaspoon dried tarragon
¼ teaspoon prepared mustard
⅛ teaspoon salt
   Nonstick cooking spray
2 lean white fish fillets* (about ¼ pound each), rinsed
   and patted dry
¼ teaspoon paprika

Cod, orange roughy, flounder, haddock, halibut and sole can be used.

1. Combine 2 teaspoons lemon juice, margarine, lemon peel, tarragon, mustard and salt in small bowl; stir until well blended. Set aside.

2. Coat 12-inch nonstick skillet with cooking spray; heat over medium heat.

3. Drizzle fillets with remaining 2 teaspoons lemon juice. Sprinkle one side of each fillet with paprika. Place fillets in skillet, paprika side down; cook 3 minutes. Gently turn and cook 3 minutes longer or until fish begins to flake when tested with fork. Place fillets on serving plates; top with margarine mixture.   *Makes 2 servings*

Nutrients per Serving (½ of total recipe):
Calories: 125, **Calories from Fat:** 24%, **Total Fat:** 3g,
Saturated Fat: 1g, **Cholesterol:** 60mg, **Sodium:** 291mg,
Carbohydrate: 1g, **Dietary Fiber:** <1g, **Protein:** 22g

Dietary Exchanges: 3 Lean Meat

Grilled Tuna Niçoise with Citrus Marinade

Citrus Marinade (page 50)
1 tuna steak (about 1 pound)
2 cups fresh green beans, trimmed and halved
4 cups romaine lettuce leaves, washed and torn
8 unpeeled small red potatoes, cooked and quartered
1 cup chopped seeded tomato
4 cooked egg whites, chopped
¼ cup red onion slices
2 teaspoons chopped black olives
Fat-free salad dressing (optional)

1. Prepare Citrus Marinade; pour into large resealable food storage bag. Add tuna; seal bag. Marinate in refrigerator 1 hour, turning occasionally.* Drain tuna; discard marinade.

2. Spray grid with nonstick cooking spray. Prepare grill for direct cooking.

3. Place tuna on grid 4 inches from hot coals. Grill 8 to 10 minutes or until tuna begins to flake when tested with fork, turning once. (Or, place tuna on rack of broiler pan coated with nonstick cooking spray. Broil 4 inches from heat 8 to 10 minutes or until tuna begins to flake when tested with fork, turning once.) Slice tuna into ¼-inch-thick slices; set aside.

4. Bring 2 cups water to a boil in large saucepan over high heat. Add beans; cook 2 minutes. Drain; rinse with cold water and drain again.

5. Place lettuce on large serving platter. Arrange tuna, beans, potatoes, tomato, egg whites and onion on lettuce. Sprinkle with olives. Serve with dressing, if desired.

Makes 4 servings

Marinate in refrigerator 1 hour for each inch of thickness.

continued on page 50

Nutrients per Serving (2 melts [2 topped English muffin halves]):
Calories: 313, **Calories from Fat:** 23%, **Total Fat:** 8g,
Saturated Fat: 2g, **Cholesterol:** 43mg, **Sodium:** 882mg,
Carbohydrate: 30g, **Dietary Fiber:** 2g, **Protein:** 30g

Dietary Exchanges: 2 Starch, 3 Lean Meat

Enlightened Jambalaya

    1 can (28 ounces) no-salt-added diced tomatoes
    1 medium onion, chopped
    1 medium red bell pepper, chopped
    1 stalk celery, chopped (about ½ cup)
    2 tablespoons minced garlic
    2 teaspoons dried parsley flakes
    2 teaspoons dried oregano
    1 teaspoon hot pepper sauce
    ½ teaspoon dried thyme
    2 pounds large raw shrimp, peeled and deveined
    1 cup uncooked instant rice
    1 cup fat-free reduced-sodium chicken broth

SLOW COOKER DIRECTIONS

1. Combine tomatoes, onion, bell pepper, celery, garlic, parsley, oregano, hot pepper sauce and thyme in slow cooker. Cover and cook on LOW 8 hours or on HIGH 4 hours. Stir in shrimp. Cover and cook on LOW 20 minutes.

2. Meanwhile, prepare rice according to package directions, substituting 1 cup chicken broth for water. Serve jambalaya over hot cooked rice.   *Makes 6 servings*

Nutrients per Serving (⅙ of total recipe):
Calories: 327, **Calories from Fat:** 9%, **Total Fat:** 3g,
Saturated Fat: <1g, **Cholesterol:** 234mg, **Sodium:** 335mg,
Carbohydrate: 37g, **Dietary Fiber:** 4g, **Protein:** 36g

Dietary Exchanges: 1½ Starch, 3 Vegetable, 4 Lean Meat

Broiled Caribbean Sea Bass

6 skinless sea bass or striped bass fillets (5 to 6 ounces each), about ½ inch thick
⅓ cup chopped fresh cilantro
2 tablespoons olive oil
2 tablespoons lime juice
2 teaspoons hot pepper sauce
2 cloves garlic, minced
1 package (7 ounces) black bean and rice mix
Lime slices (optional)

1. Place fish in shallow dish. Combine cilantro, olive oil, lime juice, hot pepper sauce and garlic in small bowl; pour over fish. Cover; marinate in refrigerator at least 30 minutes, but no longer than 2 hours.

2. Prepare black bean and rice mix according to package directions; keep warm.

3. Preheat broiler. Remove fish from marinade. Place fish on rack of broiler pan; drizzle with any remaining marinade. Broil 4 to 5 inches from heat 8 to 10 minutes or until fish is opaque. Serve fish with black beans and rice. Garnish with lime slices. *Makes 6 servings*

Nutrients per Serving (1 sea bass fillet with ½ cup black beans and rice):
Calories: 291, **Calories from Fat:** 23%, **Total Fat:** 7g, **Saturated Fat:** 1g, **Cholesterol:** 58mg, **Sodium:** 684mg, **Carbohydrate:** 25g, **Dietary Fiber:** 2g, **Protein:** 31g

Dietary Exchanges: 1½ Starch, 4 Lean Meat

Scallioned Scallops

¼ **cup all-purpose flour**
½ **teaspoon dried thyme**
½ **teaspoon paprika**
¼ **teaspoon ground red pepper**
1 **pound scallops, rinsed and patted dry**
2 **teaspoons extra-virgin olive oil**
¼ **cup finely chopped green onions**
¼ **cup dry white wine or fat-free reduced-sodium chicken broth**
2 **tablespoons lemon juice**
2 **tablespoons reduced-fat margarine**
½ **teaspoon salt**
2 **tablespoons chopped fresh parsley**

1. Combine flour, thyme, paprika and red pepper in shallow dish; stir until well blended. Add scallops and toss until well coated. Shake off excess flour; set aside.

2. Heat oil in 12-inch nonstick skillet over medium-high heat. Add scallops; cook 2 minutes. Turn scallops; cook 2 minutes or until opaque. Transfer scallops to serving platter; sprinkle with green onions.

3. Add wine and lemon juice to skillet. Bring to a boil; simmer 1 minute or until reduced slightly, scraping up browned bits from bottom and side. Remove from heat. Stir in margarine and salt until margarine is melted. Pour over scallops; sprinkle with parsley. *Makes 4 servings*

Nutrients per Serving (¼ of total recipe):
Calories: 210, **Calories from Fat:** 39%, **Total Fat:** 9g, **Saturated Fat:** <1g, **Cholesterol:** 36mg, **Sodium:** 849mg, **Carbohydrate:** 10g, **Dietary Fiber:** <1g, **Protein:** 19g

Dietary Exchanges: ½ Starch, 3 Lean Meat

meatless meals

Black Bean Tostadas

1 cup rinsed and drained canned black beans,
  mashed
2 teaspoons chili powder
  Nonstick cooking spray
4 (8-inch) corn tortillas
1 cup torn romaine lettuce leaves
1 cup chopped seeded tomato
½ cup chopped onion
½ cup plain fat-free yogurt
2 jalapeño peppers,* seeded and finely chopped

*Jalapeño peppers can sting and irritate the skin, so wear rubber
gloves when handling peppers and do not touch your eyes.

1. Combine beans and chili powder in small saucepan.
Cook over medium heat 5 minutes or until heated through,
stirring occasionally.

2. Spray large nonstick skillet with cooking spray; heat over
medium heat. Sprinkle tortillas with water; place in skillet,
1 at a time. Cook 20 to 30 seconds or until hot, turning once.

3. Spread bean mixture evenly over tortillas; layer with
lettuce, tomato, onion, yogurt and jalapeño peppers. Serve
immediately.   *Makes 4 servings*

Nutrients per Serving (1 tostada):
Calories: 146, **Calories from Fat:** 9%, **Total Fat:** 2g,
Saturated Fat: <1g, **Cholesterol:** 1mg, **Sodium:** 466mg,
Carbohydrate: 29g, **Dietary Fiber:** 5g, **Protein:** 9g

Dietary Exchanges: 1½ Starch, 1½ Vegetable

Chunky Vegetable Chili

2 tablespoons vegetable oil
1 medium onion, chopped
2 stalks celery, diced
1 carrot, diced
3 cloves garlic, minced
2 cans (about 15 ounces each) Great Northern beans,
    rinsed and drained
1½ cups water
1 cup frozen corn
1 can (6 ounces) tomato paste
1 can (4 ounces) diced mild green chiles
1 tablespoon chili powder
2 teaspoons dried oregano
1 teaspoon salt
Fresh cilantro (optional)

1. Heat oil in large skillet over medium-high heat. Add onion, celery, carrot and garlic; cook 5 minutes or until vegetables are tender, stirring occasionally.

2. Stir beans, water, corn, tomato paste, chiles, chili powder, oregano and salt into vegetable mixture in skillet. Reduce heat to medium-low. Simmer 20 minutes, stirring occasionally. Garnish with cilantro. *Makes 8 servings*

Nutrients per Serving (⅛ of total recipe):
Calories: 210, **Calories from Fat:** 17%, **Total Fat:** 4g,
Saturated Fat: <1g, **Cholesterol:** 0mg, **Sodium:** 753mg,
Carbohydrate: 36g, **Dietary Fiber:** 3g, **Protein:** 10g

Dietary Exchanges: 1½ Starch, 2 Vegetable, 1 Fat

Pan-Fried Polenta with Fresh Tomato-Bean Salsa

2½ cups chopped plum tomatoes
1 cup canned white beans, rinsed and drained
¼ cup chopped fresh basil
½ teaspoon salt
½ teaspoon black pepper
2 tablespoons olive oil, divided
1 package (16 ounces) prepared polenta, sliced into
    ¼-inch-thick rounds
¼ cup grated Parmesan cheese

1. Stir together tomatoes, beans, basil, salt and pepper. Let stand at room temperature 15 minutes to blend flavors.

2. Heat 1 tablespoon oil in medium nonstick skillet over medium-high heat. Add half of polenta slices to skillet and cook about 4 minutes or until golden brown on both sides, turning once. Remove polenta from skillet. Repeat with remaining oil and polenta slices.

3. Arrange polenta on serving plates. Top with tomato-bean mixture. Sprinkle with cheese.   *Makes 4 servings*

Nutrients per Serving (¼ of total recipe):
Calories: 234, **Calories from Fat:** 21%, **Total Fat:** 6g,
Saturated Fat: 1g, **Cholesterol:** 0mg, **Sodium:** 340mg,
Carbohydrate: 41g, **Dietary Fiber:** 14g, **Protein:** 8g

Dietary Exchanges: 2 Starch, 2 Vegetable, 1 Fat

Pan-Fried Polenta with
Fresh Tomato-Bean Salsa

Speedy Garden Roll-Ups

Chickpea Spread (recipe follows)
4 (7-inch) flour tortillas
½ cup shredded carrot
½ cup shredded red cabbage
½ cup (2 ounces) shredded reduced-fat Cheddar
cheese
4 red leaf lettuce leaves

1. Prepare Chickpea Spread. Spread each tortilla with
¼ cup Chickpea Spread to about ½ inch from edge. Sprinkle
each tortilla with 2 tablespoons *each* carrot, cabbage and
cheese. Top with 1 lettuce leaf.

2. Roll up tortillas jelly-roll style. Seal with additional
Chickpea Spread.

3. Serve immediately or wrap tightly with plastic wrap and
refrigerate up to 4 hours.   *Makes 4 servings*

Chickpea Spread

1 can (about 15 ounces) chickpeas, rinsed and drained
¼ cup fat-free cream cheese
1 tablespoon finely chopped onion
1 tablespoon chopped fresh cilantro
2 teaspoons lemon juice
2 cloves garlic
½ teaspoon sesame oil
⅛ teaspoon black pepper

Place all ingredients in food processor or blender; process
until smooth.   *Makes about 1 cup*

Nutrients per Serving (1 roll-up):
Calories: 280, **Calories from Fat:** 21%, **Total Fat:** 7g,
Saturated Fat: 2g, **Cholesterol:** 10mg, **Sodium:** 633mg,
Carbohydrate: 40g, **Dietary Fiber:** 7g, **Protein:** 15g

Dietary Exchanges: 2½ Starch, ½ Vegetable, 1 Lean Meat,
½ Fat

Nutrients per Serving (1 piece lasagna):
Calories: 273, **Calories from Fat:** 21%, **Total Fat:** 7g,
Saturated Fat: 3g, **Cholesterol:** 19mg, **Sodium:** 424mg,
Carbohydrate: 37g, **Dietary Fiber:** 6g, **Protein:** 21g

Dietary Exchanges: 1 Starch, 4 Vegetable, 2 Lean Meat

Quick Skillet Quiche

4 eggs
⅓ cup 1% milk
2 teaspoons Cajun seasoning
1 cup reduced-fat Cheddar cheese, divided
1 cup UNCLE BEN'S® Instant Rice
1 cup chopped fresh asparagus
¾ cup chopped green onions
½ cup chopped red bell pepper

1. Preheat oven to 350°F. In medium bowl, whisk eggs, milk, Cajun seasoning and ½ cup cheese. Set aside.

2. Cook rice according to package directions.

3. Meanwhile, spray medium skillet with nonstick cooking spray. Heat over medium heat until hot. Add asparagus, green onions and bell pepper. Cook and stir 5 minutes. Add rice and mix well.

4. Shape rice mixture to form crust on bottom and halfway up side of skillet. Pour egg mixture over crust. Sprinkle with remaining ½ cup cheese. Cover; cook over medium-low heat 10 minutes or until eggs are nearly set. Transfer skillet to oven and bake 5 minutes or until eggs are completely set.

Makes 6 servings

Nutrients per Serving (1 quiche wedge):
Calories: 173, **Calories from Fat:** 34%, **Total Fat:** 6g,
Saturated Fat: 3g, **Cholesterol:** 152mg, **Sodium:** 372mg,
Carbohydrate: 17g, **Dietary Fiber:** 1g, **Protein:** 11g

Dietary Exchanges: 1 Starch, 1 Vegetable, 1 Lean Meat, ½ Fat

Barley and Swiss Chard Skillet Casserole

1 cup water
¾ cup uncooked quick-cooking barley
1 cup chopped red bell pepper
1 cup chopped green bell pepper
⅛ teaspoon garlic powder
⅛ teaspoon red pepper flakes
2 cups packed finely chopped Swiss chard leaves*
1 cup rinsed and drained canned reduced-sodium navy beans
1 cup quartered cherry tomatoes (sweet grape variety)
¼ cup chopped fresh basil
1 tablespoon olive oil
2 tablespoons Italian-seasoned dry bread crumbs

*Fresh spinach or beet greens can be substituted for Swiss chard.

1. Preheat broiler.

2. Bring water to a boil in large skillet; add barley, bell peppers, garlic powder and red pepper flakes. Reduce heat; cover tightly and simmer 10 minutes or until liquid is absorbed.

3. Remove skillet from heat. Stir in chard, beans, tomatoes, basil and oil. Sprinkle evenly with bread crumbs. Broil, uncovered, 2 minutes or until golden brown.

Makes 4 servings

Nutrients per Serving (1¼ cups casserole):
Calories: 288, **Calories from Fat:** 18%, **Total Fat:** 6g,
Saturated Fat: <1g, **Cholesterol:** 0mg, **Sodium:** 488mg,
Carbohydrate: 45g, **Dietary Fiber:** 12g, **Protein:** 10g

Dietary Exchanges: 3 Starch, 1½ Fat

Black Beans & Rice Stuffed Poblano Peppers

2 large poblano peppers*
½ (15-ounce) can black beans, rinsed and drained
½ cup cooked brown rice
⅓ cup mild or medium chunky salsa
¼ cup plus 4 teaspoons shredded reduced-fat
    Cheddar cheese or pepper Jack cheese, divided

Poblano peppers can sting and irritate the skin, so wear rubber gloves when handling peppers and do not touch your eyes.

1. Preheat oven to 375°F. Lightly spray shallow baking pan with olive oil cooking spray.

2. Cut thin slice lengthwise from one side of each pepper. Chop both pepper slices; set aside. Fill medium saucepan half full with water. Bring to a boil over high heat. Add peppers; cook 6 minutes. Drain; rinse with cold water. Remove and discard seeds and membranes.

3. Stir together beans, rice, salsa, reserved chopped pepper and ¼ cup cheese in medium bowl. Spoon into peppers, mounding mixture. Place peppers in prepared pan. Cover with foil. Bake 12 to 15 minutes or until heated through.

4. Sprinkle with remaining 4 teaspoons cheese. Bake 2 minutes or until cheese melts. *Makes 2 servings*

Nutrients per Serving (1 stuffed poblano pepper):
Calories: 236, **Calories from Fat:** 15%, **Total Fat:** 4g,
Saturated Fat: 2g, **Cholesterol:** 7mg, **Sodium:** 772mg,
Carbohydrate: 38g, **Dietary Fiber:** 5g, **Protein:** 14g

Dietary Exchanges: 2 Starch, 1 Vegetable, 1 Lean Meat

Spicy Turkey Casserole

1 tablespoon olive oil
1 pound turkey breast cutlets, cut into ½-inch pieces
2 spicy turkey or chicken sausages (about 3 ounces
    each), cut into ½-inch slices
1 cup diced green bell pepper
½ cup sliced mushrooms
½ cup diced onion
1 jalapeño pepper,* seeded and minced (optional)
½ cup fat-free reduced-sodium chicken broth or water
1 can (about 14 ounces) no-salt-added diced tomatoes
1 cup cooked yolk-free egg noodles
1 teaspoon Italian seasoning
½ teaspoon paprika
¼ teaspoon black pepper
6 tablespoons grated Parmesan cheese
2 tablespoons coarse plain dry bread crumbs

*Jalapeño peppers can sting and irritate the skin, so wear rubber
gloves when handling peppers and do not touch your eyes.

1. Preheat oven to 350°F. Heat oil in large nonstick skillet
over medium heat. Add turkey and sausages; cook and stir
2 minutes. Add bell pepper, mushrooms, onion and jalapeño
pepper, if desired; cook and stir 5 minutes. Add chicken
broth; cook 1 minute, scraping up any browned bits from
bottom of skillet. Add tomatoes, noodles, seasoning, paprika
and black pepper.

2. Spoon turkey mixture into shallow 10-inch round baking
dish. Sprinkle with cheese and bread crumbs. Bake 15 to
20 minutes or until mixture is heated through and bread
crumbs are golden brown. *Makes 6 servings*

Nutrients per Serving (1 cup casserole):
Calories: 268, **Calories from Fat:** 23%, **Total Fat:** 6g,
Saturated Fat: 2g, **Cholesterol:** 52mg, **Sodium:** 347mg,
Carbohydrate: 23g, **Dietary Fiber:** 3g, **Protein:** 25g

Dietary Exchanges: 1 Starch, 1 Vegetable, 3 Lean Meat

Barbecue Chicken with Corn Bread Topper

1½ **pounds boneless skinless chicken breasts and thighs**
1 **can (about 15 ounces) red beans, rinsed and drained**
1 **can (8 ounces) tomato sauce**
1 **cup chopped green bell pepper**
½ **cup barbecue sauce**
1 **package (6 ounces) corn bread mix, plus ingredients to prepare mix**

1. Cut chicken into ¾-inch cubes. Heat large nonstick skillet over medium heat. Add chicken; cook and stir 5 minutes or until cooked through.

2. Combine chicken, beans, tomato sauce, bell pepper and barbecue sauce in 8-inch microwavable ovenproof dish.

3. Preheat oven to 375°F. Loosely cover chicken mixture with plastic wrap or waxed paper. Microwave on MEDIUM-HIGH (70%) 8 minutes or until heated through, stirring after 4 minutes.

4. Meanwhile, prepare corn bread mix according to package directions. Spoon batter over chicken mixture. Bake 15 to 18 minutes or until toothpick inserted into center of corn bread layer comes out clean.

Makes 8 servings

Nutrients per Serving (⅛ of total recipe):
Calories: 324, **Calories from Fat:** 22%, **Total Fat:** 8g,
Saturated Fat: 1g, **Cholesterol:** 51mg, **Sodium:** 781mg,
Carbohydrate: 38g, **Dietary Fiber:** 6g, **Protein:** 26g

Dietary Exchanges: 2½ Starch, 2½ Lean Meat

Barbecue Chicken with Corn Bread Topper

Grilled Salmon Fillets, Asparagus and Onions

6 salmon fillets (about 6 ounces each)
½ teaspoon paprika
⅓ cup bottled honey-Dijon marinade or barbecue sauce
1 bunch (about 1 pound) asparagus spears, tough ends trimmed
1 large red or sweet onion, cut into ¼-inch slices
1 tablespoon olive oil
¼ teaspoon salt
¼ teaspoon black pepper

1. Prepare grill for direct cooking. Place salmon in shallow dish; sprinkle with paprika. Brush marinade over salmon; marinate at room temperature 15 minutes.

2. Brush asparagus and onion slices with olive oil; season with salt and pepper.

3. Place salmon, skin side down, in center of oiled grid over medium coals. Arrange asparagus spears and onion slices around salmon. Grill salmon and vegetables on covered grill 10 minutes, turning once, or until salmon begins to flake when tested with a fork and vegetables are crisp-tender. Separate onion slices into rings. Serve salmon with asparagus and onion. *Makes 6 servings*

Prep and Cook Time: 26 minutes

Nutrients per Serving (1 salmon fillet with ¾ cup asparagus and onion mixture):
Calories: 255, **Calories from Fat:** 30%, **Total Fat:** 8g, **Saturated Fat:** 1g, **Cholesterol:** 86mg, **Sodium:** 483mg, **Carbohydrate:** 8g, **Dietary Fiber:** 2g, **Protein:** 35g

Dietary Exchanges: 1 Vegetable, 4 Lean Meat

Turkey Sausage & Pasta Toss

8 ounces uncooked penne or gemelli pasta
1 can (about 14 ounces) no-salt-added stewed tomatoes
6 ounces turkey kielbasa or smoked turkey sausage, cut into ¼-inch slices
2 cups (1-inch) asparagus pieces or broccoli florets
2 tablespoons reduced-fat pesto
2 tablespoons grated Parmesan cheese

1. Cook pasta according to package directions, omitting salt. Drain; keep warm.

2. Meanwhile, heat tomatoes in medium saucepan over medium heat; add turkey kielbasa. Stir in asparagus and pesto; cover and simmer about 6 minutes or until asparagus is crisp-tender.

3. Toss pasta with tomato mixture; sprinkle with cheese.

Makes 4 servings

Prep and Cook Time: 25 minutes

Nutrients per Serving (¼ of total recipe):
Calories: 342, **Calories from Fat:** 18%, **Total Fat:** 7g,
Saturated Fat: 2g, **Cholesterol:** 30mg, **Sodium:** 483mg,
Carbohydrate: 53g, **Dietary Fiber:** 5g, **Protein:** 18g

Dietary Exchanges: 3 Starch, 1 Vegetable, 2 Lean Meat

Turkey is naturally low in fat, making it a great substitute for pork and beef in some favorite indulgences, like bacon and sausage. You can find these turkey products in most large supermarkets.

Turkey Sausage & Pasta Toss

Crispy Oven-Baked Chicken

4 boneless skinless chicken breasts (about 4 ounces each)

¾ cup GUILTLESS GOURMET® Roasted Red Pepper Salsa

Nonstick cooking spray

1 cup (3.5 ounces) crushed* GUILTLESS GOURMET® Baked Tortilla Chips (yellow corn, red corn or chili lime)

Cherry tomatoes and pineapple sage leaves (optional)

*Crush tortilla chips in the original bag or between two pieces of waxed paper with a rolling pin.

Wash chicken; pat dry with paper towels. Place chicken in shallow nonmetal pan or place in large resealable plastic food storage bag. Pour salsa over chicken. Cover with foil or seal bag; marinate in refrigerator 8 hours or overnight.

Preheat oven to 350°F. Coat baking sheet with cooking spray. Place crushed chips on waxed paper. Remove chicken from salsa, discarding salsa; roll chicken in crushed chips. Place on prepared baking sheet; bake 45 minutes or until chicken is no longer pink in center and chips are crisp. Serve hot. Garnish with tomatoes and sage, if desired.

Makes 4 servings

Nutrients per Serving (1 Crispy Oven-Baked Chicken breast):
Calories: 245, **Calories from Fat:** 18%, **Total Fat:** 5g,
Saturated Fat: 1g, **Cholesterol:** 69mg, **Sodium:** 272mg,
Carbohydrate: 21g, **Dietary Fiber:** 2g, **Protein:** 27g

Dietary Exchanges: 1½ Starch, 3 Lean Meat

Pan Seared Halibut Steaks with Avocado Salsa

4 tablespoons chipotle salsa, divided
½ teaspoon salt, divided
4 small (4- to 5-ounce) *or* 2 large (8- to 10-ounce)
    halibut steaks, cut ¾ inch thick
½ cup diced tomato
½ ripe avocado, diced
2 tablespoons chopped fresh cilantro (optional)
    Lime wedges (optional)

1. Combine 2 tablespoons salsa and ¼ teaspoon salt; spread over both sides of halibut.

2. Heat large nonstick skillet over medium heat. Add halibut; cook 4 to 5 minutes per side or until fish begins to flake when tested with fork.

3. For Avocado Salsa, combine remaining 2 tablespoons salsa, ¼ teaspoon salt, tomato, avocado and cilantro, if desired, in small bowl. Mix well and spoon over cooked fish. Garnish with lime wedges. *Makes 4 servings*

Nutrients per Serving (1 cooked small [or ½ cooked large] halibut steak with about 3 tablespoons Avocado Salsa):
Calories: 169, **Calories from Fat:** 36%, **Total Fat:** 7g, **Saturated Fat:** <1g, **Cholesterol:** 36mg, **Sodium:** 476mg, **Carbohydrate:** 2g, **Dietary Fiber:** 4g, **Protein:** 25g

Dietary Exchanges: 3 Lean Meat

Mediterranean Pork Pocket Sandwiches

¾ **pound boneless lean top loin pork chops (¾ inch thick)**
⅓ **cup fat-free Italian Caesar salad dressing**
1 **cup finely chopped seeded cucumber**
⅓ **cup plain fat-free yogurt**
¼ **cup finely chopped red onion**
2 **(6-inch) rounds whole wheat pita bread, cut in half**

1. Preheat oven to 450°F. Spray shallow baking pan with nonstick cooking spray; set aside.

2. Cut pork into thin strips. Place in medium bowl. Drizzle with salad dressing; toss to coat.

3. Spread pork mixture in single layer in prepared baking pan. Bake 10 to 12 minutes or until meat starts to brown.

4. Meanwhile, combine cucumber, yogurt and red onion in medium bowl; toss. Spoon meat and cucumber mixture into pita halves.   *Makes 4 servings*

Hint: For cold sandwiches, chill the meat and cucumber mixtures in separate containers, then fill pita halves or wrap in whole wheat tortillas.

Nutrients per Serving (1 sandwich [1 stuffed pita half]):
Calories: 209, **Calories from Fat:** 13%, **Total Fat:** 3g,
Saturated Fat: 572g, **Cholesterol:** 47mg, **Sodium:** 578mg,
Carbohydrate: 21g, **Dietary Fiber:** 3g, **Protein:** 24g

Dietary Exchanges: 1 Starch, 1 Vegetable, 2 Lean Meat

Easy Cheesy Ham and Veggie Rice Casserole

1 packet (3½ ounces) boil-in-a-bag brown rice
2 cups broccoli florets
1 cup (3 ounces) matchstick-size carrot strips
6 ounces lean reduced-sodium ham, diced
2 ounces Swiss cheese, broken into small pieces
¾ cup (3 ounces) shredded reduced-fat sharp Cheddar
    cheese, divided
1 tablespoon trans-fat-free reduced-calorie margarine
⅛ teaspoon ground red pepper

1. Cook rice in large saucepan according to package directions, omitting salt and fat. Remove rice packet when cooked; reserve water.

2. Add broccoli and carrots to water in saucepan; bring to a boil over high heat. Reduce heat; cover and simmer 3 minutes or until broccoli is crisp-tender.

3. Drain vegetables. Return vegetables and cooked rice to saucepan; heat over medium-low heat. Add ham, Swiss, one third of Cheddar, margarine and red pepper; stir gently. Sprinkle evenly with remaining Cheddar; cover and cook 3 minutes or until cheese melts.   *Makes 4 servings*

Nutrients per Serving (1½ cups casserole):
Calories: 283, **Calories from Fat:** 38%, **Total Fat:** 12g,
Saturated Fat: 6g, **Cholesterol:** 48mg, **Sodium:** 616mg,
Carbohydrate: 26g, **Dietary Fiber:** 2g, **Protein:** 19g

Dietary Exchanges: 1½ Starch, 1 Vegetable, 2 Lean Meat, 1 Fat

Hot Chinese Chicken Salad

8 ounces fresh or steamed Chinese egg noodles
¼ cup fat-free reduced-sodium chicken broth
2 tablespoons rice wine vinegar
2 tablespoons reduced-sodium soy sauce
1 tablespoon rice wine or dry sherry
1 teaspoon sugar
½ teaspoon red pepper flakes
3 teaspoons vegetable oil, divided
1½ cups snow peas, diagonally sliced
1 cup thinly sliced green or red bell pepper
1 clove garlic, minced
1 pound boneless skinless chicken breasts, cut
   into bite-size pieces
1 cup thinly sliced red or green cabbage
2 green onions, thinly sliced

1. Cook noodles in boiling water 4 to 5 minutes or until tender. Drain; set aside. Combine chicken broth, vinegar, soy sauce, rice wine, sugar and red pepper flakes in small bowl; set aside.

2. Heat 1 teaspoon oil in wok or large nonstick skillet. Add snow peas, bell pepper and garlic; stir-fry 1 to 2 minutes or until vegetables are crisp-tender. Remove from wok; set aside.

3. Heat remaining 2 teaspoons oil in wok. Add chicken; stir-fry 3 to 4 minutes or until chicken is cooked through. Add cabbage, cooked vegetables and noodles. Stir in broth mixture; toss until well blended. Cook and stir 1 to 2 minutes or until heated through. Sprinkle with green onions before serving.   *Makes 6 servings*

Nutrients per Serving (1⅓ cups salad):
Calories: 241, **Calories from Fat:** 14%, **Total Fat:** 4g,
Saturated Fat: 1g, **Cholesterol:** 45mg, **Sodium:** 419mg,
Carbohydrate: 27g, **Dietary Fiber:** 3g, **Protein:** 23g

Dietary Exchanges: 1½ Starch, 1 Vegetable, 2 Lean Meat

Turkey-Tortilla Bake

9 (6-inch) corn tortillas
½ pound 93% lean ground turkey
½ cup chopped onion
¾ cup mild or medium taco sauce
1 can (4 ounces) chopped mild green chiles, drained
½ cup frozen corn, thawed
½ cup (2 ounces) shredded reduced-fat Cheddar
cheese
Fat-free or reduced-fat sour cream (optional)

1. Preheat oven to 400°F. Place tortillas on large baking sheet, overlapping as little as possible; bake 4 minutes. Turn tortillas; bake 2 minutes or until crisp. Cool completely on wire rack.

2. Heat medium nonstick skillet over medium heat. Add turkey and onion. Cook and stir 5 minutes or until turkey is browned and onion is tender. Add taco sauce, chiles and corn. Reduce heat and simmer 5 minutes.

3. Break 3 tortillas and arrange over bottom of 1½-quart casserole. Spoon half of turkey mixture over tortillas; sprinkle with half of cheese. Repeat layers. Bake 10 minutes or until cheese is melted and casserole is heated through. Break remaining 3 tortillas into pieces and sprinkle over casserole. Cut into 4 wedges. Garnish with sour cream.

Makes 4 servings

Prep and Cook Time: 30 minutes

Nutrients per Serving (1 wedge):
Calories: 279, **Calories from Fat:** 25%, **Total Fat:** 8g,
Saturated Fat: 2g, **Cholesterol:** 26mg, **Sodium:** 666mg,
Carbohydrate: 38g, **Dietary Fiber:** 1g, **Protein:** 17g

Dietary Exchanges: 2½ Starch, 1 Lean Meat, 1 Fat

index
· · · · · ·

index & acknowledgments

The publisher would like to thank the companies and organizations listed below for the use of their recipes and photographs in this publication.

Guiltless Gourmet®

MASTERFOODS USA

National Honey Board